WHAT BLOSSOMS IN SPRING?

by Jenna Lee Gleisner

Cherry Lake Publishing • Ann Arbor, Michigan

Published in the United States of America
by Cherry Lake Publishing
Ann Arbor, Michigan
www.cherrylakepublishing.com

Consultant: Marla Conn, ReadAbility, Inc.

Photo Credits: Shutterstock Images, Cover, Title, 8, 16, 18, 20; Dmitriy Yakovlev/Shutterstock Images, 4; Vira Mylyan-Monastyrska/Shutterstock Images, 6; Maryna Pleshkun/Shutterstock Images, 10; Pierre Leclerc/Shutterstock Images, 12; Alena Ozerova/Shutterstock Images, 14

Library of Congress Cataloging-in-Publication Data
Gleisner, Jenna Lee.
  What blossoms in spring? / by Jenna Lee Gleisner.
    p. cm. -- (Let's look at spring)
Audience: 5-7.
Audience: K to grade 3.
Includes index.
  ISBN 978-1-62431-659-3 (hardcover) -- ISBN 978-1-62431-686-9 (pbk.) -- ISBN 978-1-62431-713-2 (pdf) -- ISBN 978-1-62431-740-8 (hosted ebook)
  1. Plants, Flowering of--Juvenile literature. 2. Flowers--Juvenile literature. 3. Spring--Juvenile literature. I. Title. II. Series: Gleisner, Jenna Lee. Let's look at spring.

QK830.G54 2015
582.13--dc23

2013029053

Cherry Lake Publishing would like to acknowledge the work of The Partnership for 21st Century Skills. Please visit *www.p21.org* for more information.

Printed in the United States of America
Corporate Graphics Inc.
January 2014

TABLE OF CONTENTS

Spring Season

Spring is here. Days get warmer. New plants begin to grow.

Lots of rain falls. Rain and sunlight help **buds** grow.

What Do You See?

What color tulips do you see?

Flowers

Buds **blossom**. They turn into flowers. Tulips blossom every spring.

What Do You See?

What insect do you see on the apple tree blossom?

Apple trees blossom. The flowers will turn into fruit.

Water lilies grow in ponds.
They blossom on top of the
water.

Poppies blossom. They grow in fields. Mel picks poppies.

What Do You See?

Are the lilacs Jill smells purple, pink, or white?

Petals

Jill smells lilacs. Lilac **petals** are purple, pink, or white.

Dandelions have tiny yellow petals. They will turn into white seeds.

Spring Ends

Plants blossom all spring long. What season comes next?

Find Out More

BOOK
Aloian, Molly. *How Do We Know It's Spring?* New York: Crabtree, 2013.

WEB SITE
Spring Match Game
www.primarygames.com/season_match/spring_match /spring_match.htm
Match up your favorite spring items to reveal a spring flower.

Glossary

blossom (BLAH-suhm) to grow

buds (BUHDZ) small bumps on a plant that grow into leaves or flowers

petals (PET-uhlz) the colored parts on the outside of a flower

Home and School Connection

Use this list of words from the book to help your child become a better reader. Word games and writing activities can help beginning readers reinforce literacy skills.

apple	grow	poppies	tiny
blossom	lilacs	purple	trees
buds	lilies	rain	tulips
dandelion	petals	season	warmer
days	pick	seeds	water
fields	pink	smell	white
flowers	plants	spring	yellow
fruit	ponds	sunlight	

What Do You See?

What Do You See? is a feature paired with select photos in this book. It encourages young readers to interact with visual images in order to build the ability to integrate content in various media formats.

You can help your child further evaluate photos in this book with additional activities. Look at the images in the book without the What Do You See? feature. Ask your child to point out one detail in each image, such as a color, time of day, animal, or setting.

Index

About the Author

Jenna Lee Gleisner is an editor and author who lives in Minnesota. She loves when spring comes to Minnesota and new buds appear on the trees. Her favorite spring plant is the lilac because of its sweet smell!